Over-the-Counter Drugs

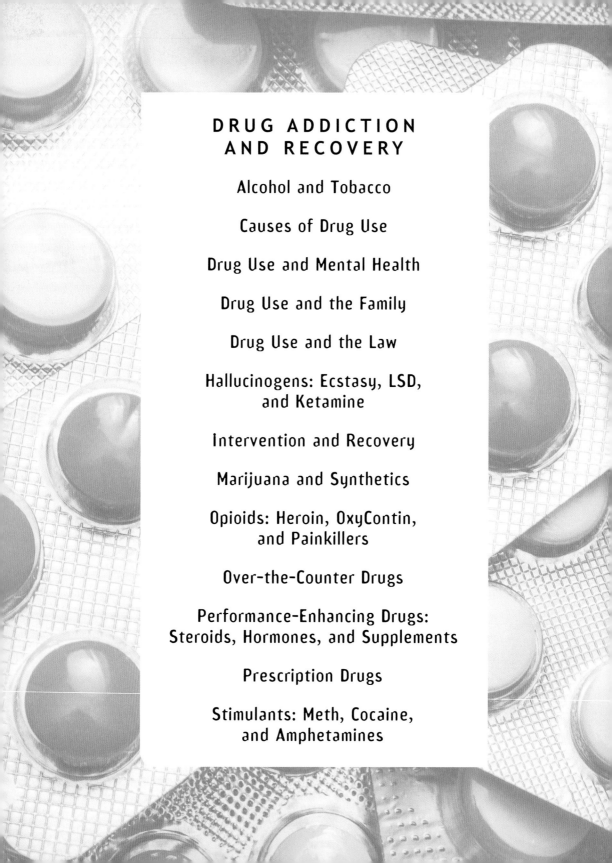

DRUG ADDICTION AND RECOVERY

Over-the-Counter Drugs

H.W. Poole

SERIES CONSULTANT
SARA BECKER, Ph.D.
Brown University School of Public Health
Warren Alpert Medical School

Fountaindale Public Library
Bolingbrook, IL
(630) 759-2102

MASON CREST

Mason Crest
450 Parkway Drive, Suite D
Broomall, PA 19008
www.masoncrest.com

MTM Publishing, Inc.
www.mtmpublishing.com

President: Valerie Tomaselli
Vice President, Book Development: Hilary Poole
Designer: Annemarie Redmond
Copyeditor: Peter Jaskowiak
Editorial Assistant: Andrea St. Aubin

Series ISBN: 978-1-4222-3598-0
Hardback ISBN: 978-1-4222-3608-6
E-Book ISBN: 978-1-4222-8252-6

Cataloging-in-Publication Data on file with the Library of Congress

Printed and bound in the United States of America.

First printing
9 8 7 6 5 4 3 2 1

QR CODES AND LINKS TO THIRD PARTY CONTENT

TABLE OF CONTENTS

Key Icons to Look for:

Words to Understand: These words with their easy-to-understand definitions will increase the reader's understanding of the text, while building vocabulary skills.

Sidebars: This boxed material within the main text allows readers to build knowledge, gain insights, explore possibilities, and broaden their perspectives by weaving together additional information to provide realistic and holistic perspectives.

Research Projects: Readers are pointed toward areas of further inquiry connected to each chapter. Suggestions are provided for projects that encourage deeper research and analysis.

Text-Dependent Questions: These questions send the reader back to the text for more careful attention to the evidence presented there.

Educational Videos: Readers can view videos by scanning our QR codes, providing them with additional educational content to supplement the text. Examples include news coverage, moments in history, speeches, iconic sports moments and much more!

Series Glossary of Key Terms: This back-of-the-book glossary contains terminology used throughout the series. Words found here increase the reader's ability to read and comprehend higher-level books and articles in this field.

SERIES INTRODUCTION

Many adolescents in the United States will experiment with alcohol or other drugs by time they finish high school. According to a 2014 study funded by the National Institute on Drug Abuse, about 27 percent of 8th graders have tried alcohol, 20 percent have tried drugs, and 13 percent have tried cigarettes. By 12th grade, these rates more than double: 66 percent of 12th graders have tried alcohol, 50 percent have tried drugs, and 35 percent have tried cigarettes.

Adolescents who use substances experience an increased risk of a wide range of negative consequences, including physical injury, family conflict, school truancy, legal problems, and sexually transmitted diseases. Higher rates of substance use are also associated with the leading causes of death in this age group: accidents, suicide, and violent crime. Relative to adults, adolescents who experiment with alcohol or other drugs progress more quickly to a full-blown substance use disorder and have more co-occurring mental health problems.

The National Survey on Drug Use and Health (NSDUH) estimated that in 2015 about 1.3 million adolescents between the ages of 12 and 17 (5 percent of adolescents in the United States) met the medical criteria for a substance use disorder. Unfortunately, the vast majority of these

IF YOU NEED HELP NOW . . .

SAMHSA's National Helpline provides referrals for mental-health or substance-use counseling.
1-800-662-HELP (4357) or https://findtreatment.samhsa.gov

SAMHSA's National Suicide Prevention Lifeline provides crisis counseling by phone or online, 24-hours-a-day and 7 days a week.
1-800-273-TALK (8255) or http://www.suicidepreventionlifeline.org

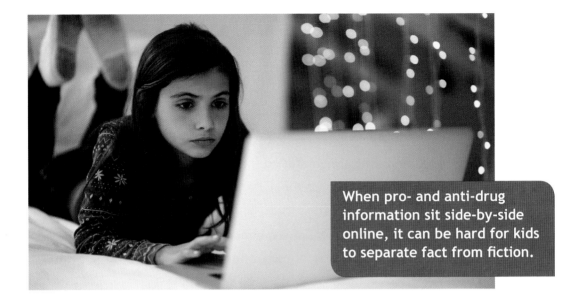

When pro- and anti-drug information sit side-by-side online, it can be hard for kids to separate fact from fiction.

adolescents did not receive treatment. Less than 10 percent of those with a diagnosis received specialty care, leaving 1.2 million adolescents with an unmet need for treatment.

The NSDUH asked the 1.2 million adolescents with untreated substance use disorders why they didn't receive specialty care. Over 95 percent said that they didn't think they needed it. The other 5 percent reported challenges finding quality treatment that was covered by their insurance. Very few treatment providers and agencies offer substance use treatment designed to meet the specific needs of adolescents. Meanwhile, numerous insurance plans have "opted out" of providing coverage for addiction treatment, while others have placed restrictions on what is covered.

Stigma about substance use is another serious problem. We don't call a person with an eating disorder a "food abuser," but we use terms like "drug abuser" to describe individuals with substance use disorders. Even treatment providers often unintentionally use judgmental words, such as describing urine screen results as either "clean" or "dirty." Underlying this language is the idea that a substance use disorder is some kind of moral failing or character flaw, and that people with these disorders deserve blame or punishment for their struggles.

And punish we do. A 2010 report by CASA Columbia found that in the United States, 65 percent of the 2.3 million people in prisons and jails met medical criteria for a substance use disorder, while another 20 percent had histories of substance use disorders, committed their crimes while under the influence of alcohol or drugs, or committed a substance-related crime. Many of these inmates spend decades in prison, but only 11 percent of them receive any treatment during their incarceration. Our society invests significantly more money in punishing individuals with substance use disorders than we do in treating them.

At a basic level, the ways our society approaches drugs and alcohol—declaring a "war on drugs," for example, or telling kids to "Just Say No!"—reflect a misunderstanding about the nature of addiction. The reality is that addiction is a disease that affects all types of people—parents and children, rich and poor, young and old. Substance use disorders stem from a complex interplay of genes, biology, and the environment, much like most physical and mental illnesses.

The way we talk about recovery, using phrases like "kick the habit" or "breaking free," also misses the mark. Substance use disorders are chronic, insidious, and debilitating illnesses. Fortunately, there are a number of effective treatments for substance use disorders. For many patients, however, the road is long and hard. Individuals recovering from substance use disorders can experience horrible withdrawal symptoms, and many will continue to struggle with cravings for alcohol or drugs. It can be a daily struggle to cope with these cravings and stay abstinent. A popular saying at Alcoholics Anonymous (AA) meetings is "one day at a time," because every day of recovery should be respected and celebrated.

There are a lot of incorrect stereotypes about individuals with substance use disorders, and there is a lot of false information about the substances, too. If you do an Internet search on the term "marijuana," for instance, two top hits are a web page by the National Institute on Drug Abuse and a page operated by Weedmaps, a medical and recreational marijuana dispensary. One of these pages publishes scientific information and one publishes pro-marijuana articles. Both pages have a high-quality, professional appearance. If you had never heard of either organization, it would be hard to know which to trust. It can be really difficult for the average person, much less the average teenager, to navigate these waters.

The topics covered in this series were specifically selected to be relevant to teenagers. About half of the volumes cover the types of drugs that they are most likely to hear about or to come in contact with. The other half cover important issues related to alcohol and other drug use (which we refer to as "drug use" in the titles for simplicity). These books cover topics such as the causes of drug use, the influence of drug use on the family, drug use and the legal system, drug use and mental health, and treatment options. Many teens will either have personal experience with these issues or will know someone who does.

This series was written to help young people get the facts about common drugs, substance use disorders, substance-related problems, and recovery. Accurate information can help adolescents to make better decisions. Students who are educated can help each other to better understand the risks and consequences of drug use. Facts also go a long way to reducing the stigma associated with substance use. We tend to fear or avoid things that we don't understand. Knowing the facts can make it easier to support each other. For students who know someone struggling with a substance use disorder, these books can also help them know what to expect. If they are worried about someone, or even about themselves, these books can help to provide some answers and a place to start.

—Sara J. Becker, Ph.D., Assistant Professor (Research), Center for Alcohol and Addictions Studies, Brown University School of Public Health, Assistant Professor (Research), Department of Psychiatry and Human Behavior, Brown University Medical School

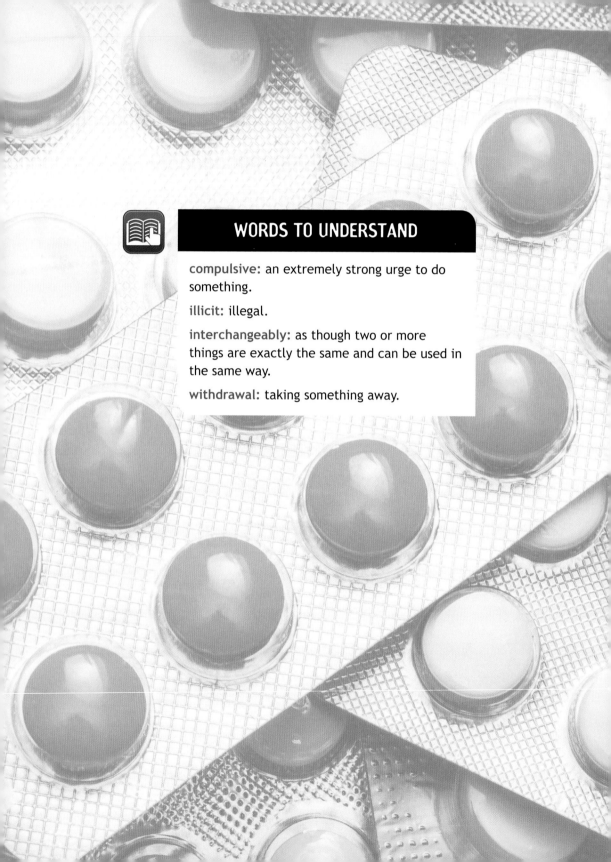

WORDS TO UNDERSTAND

compulsive: an extremely strong urge to do something.

illicit: illegal.

interchangeably: as though two or more things are exactly the same and can be used in the same way.

withdrawal: taking something away.

CHAPTER ONE

WHAT ARE OTC DRUGS?

A shifty young man paces in a dingy alley. In his hand, he has 20 dollars that he stole from an elderly neighbor. He's waiting impatiently for his dealer to arrive, but he's worried the cops may show up first. . . .

This is the stereotypical image of a drug user. It's not totally wrong—those people do exist. But consider these images, too:

- A mother of three buys another bottle of cough syrup; she's not sure why the medicine keeps disappearing from the medicine cabinet.
- A young wrestler buys a bottle of dietary supplements off the Internet, hoping against hope that they will help him finally make varsity this year.
- A cheerleader swallows yet another handful of diet pills, even though anyone can see she's dangerously underweight already.
- A lonesome kid shoplifts yet another whipped cream can from the corner store. His mom is working the third shift tonight, so she'll never know what he's up to.

These examples all involve drug use, too, but the drugs of choice come from grocery stores, pharmacies, and the Internet. Some are genuine medications that are being used in ways not listed on the bottle. Some were never intended to be used as drugs at all. But they are all legal to purchase, and for this reason, they are grouped together as "over-the-counter" (OTC) drugs.

In real life, the misuse of drugs doesn't always look the way it does in the movies.

OTC VERSUS PRESCRIPTION

Nearly everyone has had the experience of getting sick, seeing a doctor and being given a prescription, and then going to a pharmacy to pick up the medicine. But it hasn't always been this way. Legislation in 1951 called the Durham-Humphrey Amendment first created the distinction between drugs that anyone could buy and those that are available only with a prescription. Drugs that anyone can buy came to be known as over-the-counter drugs because all the buyer had to do was pay for them at the drug- or grocery-store counter.

In the context of substance use disorders, the concept of OTC has also expanded slightly, to encompass products that are used as drugs even though they are not intended to be used that way. For example, inhalants produce fumes that some people use to get high. Things like whipped cream cans and paint thinner are discussed in this volume because they can technically be bought "over the counter"—just not a pharmacy counter. As with cough medicine, some of these products are age restricted because of concerns about misuse.

MISUSE, DEPENDENCE, AND ADDICTION

In daily life, people often use the terms *drug misuse*, *dependence*, and *addiction* interchangeably. But in medicine, they are different. When it comes to OTC drugs, *misuse* just means that the person is taking the drug in a way that it was not intended to be used. In other words, they are taking too much of the drug, taking it too frequently, or taking for incorrect reasons, such as to get high rather than to cure a cough. Any substance can be misused. For example some people misuse OTC painkillers like aspirin and ibuprofen. Those drugs do not have a mood-altering effect, of course, but sometimes people take more than the recommended amount, and this does count as "misuse."

About 54 percent of Americans drink coffee every day.

Dependence is a physical condition in which someone's body relies on a particular thing (a drug in this case) in order to be "normal." For example, someone with diabetes is dependent on a medicine called insulin. Of course, that doesn't make the person a "drug addict," it just means that the person's body does not make enough insulin on its own, so medication is used to keep the person healthy.

Picture someone who says, "I can't start my day without my cup of coffee." If the person doesn't get her coffee, she will probably feel irritable and have trouble concentrating; she may have a headache or feel unwell. That person is dependent on the caffeine in coffee, and if the caffeine is taken away, she will experience withdrawal symptoms. Withdrawal can be unpleasant but minor, as with caffeine dependence, or it can be terribly painful and even life-threatening (as it is with both heroin and alcohol).

Addiction is an umbrella term that relates to the compulsive need for the particular chemical. People who are addicted to a drug will continue to use it even when facing severe negative consequences. They might get kicked out of school or lose their jobs. They might steal or do other things to get the drug that they would never ordinarily consider doing. Pursuit of the drug takes over everything else. From a treatment perspective, physical dependence is comparatively easy to treat—doctors have drugs that can ease the misery of withdrawal systems and help the body return to "normal" functioning. Treating addiction requires a much broader approach—for more on this, see the volume *Intervention and Recovery* in this set.

UNDERSTANDING OTC MISUSE

When researchers want to understand how many people are using a particular illicit drug, they have a number of different sources of information. They can look at the number of people who get arrested, for example, or at the number of people in various addiction centers. Many of these research tools are not available when it comes to OTC drug misuse. How do you figure out who is buying cough medicine because they want to misuse it, rather than those who just have the flu?

One way researchers figure this out is with a survey. Monitoring the Future (MTF) is a joint project of the National Institute on Drug Abuse and the University of Michigan. MTF has been

Regulations on OTC drugs are always evolving, as governments try to keep up with trends in use and misuse.

looking at drug use among teenagers and young adults since 1975. This survey suggests that rates of OTC misuse generally decreased between 2007 and 2014 (see the table on this page). One trouble with surveys, of course, is that you have to count on the respondents to answer truthfully. Sometimes researchers suspect that the usage of certain drugs is actually higher than surveys suggest, simply because kids may be reluctant to be honest. Interestingly, there are other moments when researchers worry that the numbers actually overestimate use, because sometimes kids misunderstand the question. For example, they may lump OTC drugs in with prescription drugs because they don't quite understand the distinction.

Another challenge for people who study OTC misuse is that the line between OTC and prescription use can get fuzzy. For one thing, laws are always evolving. Also, laws vary by state, so what is true in one area may not be true in another. Last but not least, people who are dependent on medications often take what they can get—this means they may switch back and forth between OTC and prescription medications, depending on what

TRENDS IN ANNUAL USE OF PARTICULAR DRUGS:
By Grade Level (percentage)

OTC Cough and Cold Medicines

Year	2007	2008	2009	2010	2011	2012	2013	2014
8th grade	4.0	3.6	3.8	3.2	2.7	3.0	2.9	2.0
10th grade	5.4	5.3	6.0	5.1	5.5	4.7	4.3	3.7
12th grade	5.8	5.5	5.9	6.6	5.3	5.6	5.0	4.1

Inhalants

Year	2007	2008	2009	2010	2011	2012	2013	2014
8th grade	8.3	8.9	8.1	8.1	7.0	6.2	5.2	5.3
10th grade	6.6	5.9	6.1	5.7	4.5	4.1	3.5	3.3
12th grade	3.7	3.8	3.4	3.6	3.2	2.9	2.5	1.9

Source: Monitoring the Future, 2014. http://www.monitoringthefuture.org/.

happens to be available at the moment. People might start out misusing cough syrup but then move on to "harder" painkillers and even heroin.

Kids are often tempted to experiment with OTC drugs simply because they are so easily available. Every bathroom has a medicine cabinet, and it's understandable why some kids might get curious about what's in it. But just because OTC drugs are considered safe when used properly, that does not make them safe in every instance. This is why it's so important to know the facts about OTC drugs; even many parents don't realize how many powerful chemicals are just sitting in their homes unattended.

TEXT-DEPENDENT QUESTIONS

1. What is the difference between OTC and prescription drugs?
2. Are there any restrictions on buying certain OTC drugs? What are they, and why do they exist?
3. Explain the difference between the terms *misuse*, *addiction*, and *dependence*.

RESEARCH PROJECT

Dig deeper into the statistics from the Monitoring the Future report. What trends do you notice in OTC drug use over time? What age groups are most affected? What trends do you notice in inhalant use over time, by age? (The full report is available online at http://www.monitoringthefuture.org.)

WORDS TO UNDERSTAND

depressant: something that reduces activity.

dissociative: a state of feeling disconnected from reality.

impaired: weakened or not functioning as usual.

opioid: a class of drugs that are either derived from the opium plant or made in a lab to mimic opium's effects.

stimulant: something that increases activity.

CHAPTER TWO

COUGH AND COLD MEDICINES

In a world that has eradicated smallpox and largely eliminated polio, it seems amazing that we are helpless in the face of sniffles. But it's true: there is no cure for the common cold. That doesn't mean, however, that there aren't shelves upon shelves of products that promise relief, and they are part of almost every medicine cabinet in the United States. The result, unfortunately, is that these medications are also among the easiest for kids and teens to find and misuse.

CODEINE COUGH SYRUP

The association between cough medicine and drug misuse goes back a very long time. Beginning in the late 18th century, popular cough medicines were made with heroin, a strong, highly addictive opioid. The medicines were quite popular—in 1905, for example, heroin sales made up about 5 percent of the Bayer pharmaceutical company's profits. Reports began to

Cold and cough medicines are an $8 billion industry.

surface that "addicts" were craving increasingly large amounts of the stuff around 1899. But heroin continued to be used in cough medicines until the early 1920s.

Today, many cough medicines contain small amounts of codeine, which is also an opioid, but a safer formulation of the same chemical compounds found in heroin. Codeine was created by a French chemist in the 1830s, and it has gone on to be one of the most-used medicines in the world. In the United States, codeine is mostly available only by prescription, although in some states it is legal for people over 18 to buy small doses of codeine cough syrup. In Canada, a blend of codeine and acetaminophen (Tylenol) can be purchased over the counter.

Although codeine cough syrups are far milder than the old-time heroin ones, they are still addictive, and they can sicken or even kill you if take too much. Codeine—just like heroin and other popular opioids —is a central nervous system (CNS) depressant. That means it slows down bodily functions like heart rate and breathing. While opioids are very useful for managing pain, if the drugs are taken incorrectly, they leave users vulnerable to coma or death. Unfortunately, this hasn't really prevented them from being misused.

DXM

Codeine cough syrups have been popular for a long time, but in recent years, another type of cough medication has become much more popular: dextromethorphan (DXM, or sometimes DM). DXM was first invented in the late 1950s. It is effective against a number of different cold symptoms—coughing especially, but also sinus congestion, runny nose, and sneezing. DXM is an ingredient in a huge number of cough and cold medicines, and it is very safe when used correctly. (Typical dosages are 10 to 20 milligrams every 4 hours, or 30 milligrams every 6 to 8 hours.)

When taken in high dosages, DXM can cause hallucinations and a dissociative state of mind, somewhat like LSD. Sometimes DXM comes in red pills that are referred to as "Triple C," a nickname that comes from a particular brand of cold pills. The effects are dose dependent, meaning that the more someone takes, the stronger the effects will be. Many users report experiencing a sense of euphoria when on DXM, but at the extreme end, users have also exhibited psychotic behavior. Side effects include blurred vision, sweating, lack of coordination, stomach pain, nausea and vomiting, dizziness, and drowsiness. At higher doses, other symptoms include numbness in fingers and toes, elevated heart rate, difficulty breathing, visual and auditory hallucinations, heart attack, and seizure.

There have long been reports of DXM-based products being misused. In fact, one of the first DXM cold medications was taken off the market in the 1970s due to misuse. But as codeine and alcohol were removed from cold medications because of safety concerns, they were replaced with DXM.

THE TROUBLE WITH MIXING

In the music community of Houston in the 1950s, a popular drink was made from mixing beer and Robitussin cough syrup (which, at the time, contained codeine and was sold OTC). The recipe has evolved and changed over the years—the contemporary version is called "Purple Drank" or "sirrup." It became very popular with rappers and DJs in the Houston area, and then spread far beyond that city.

Purple Drank contains codeine, but in much higher doses than would be used in medical situations. The syrup usually contains high doses of another drug, too, called promethazine, which is an antinausea medicine that has depressive properties. Both drugs are legitimate medicines when used correctly, but when combined in high doses, they magnify each other. People have been hospitalized and even died due to overdosing on these drinks. This highlights an important aspect of OTC drug misuse: sometimes the problem has less to do with any single ingredient and more to do with the combination of multiple chemicals put into one product.

But then it gets worse. After all, people don't usually consume Purple Drank when they are sitting at home alone. They take it when they are partying, which often means that alcohol (another depressant) has been added to the mix. (Energy drinks are also used in this way: this is discussed more in chapter three.) As a result, people end up ingesting dangerous doses of multiple drugs within a short period.

Purple Drank began as a drug in the Houston music scene.

In recent years, DXM misuse has reached epidemic levels: one survey suggested that 1 in 10 American teenagers had used DXM, Triple C, or similar products to get high.

There is not a lot of research available on DXM addiction. Repeated experimentation leads to physical tolerance, in which users need to take increasingly high dosages to get the same effect. Users can also become psychologically tolerant, believing firmly that they need DXM in order to feel happy, have a good time,

Many schools forbid students from bringing cold medication with them, because administrators are worried about misuse.

and so on. A survey of a number of DXM users published in 2007 found that just under half of them exhibited psychological signs of dependence, such as depression and insomnia when the drug was removed. Signs of physical dependence have also been noted in a case study published by the *Journal of the American Board of Family Medicine*. Other research suggests that DXM misuse can be a "gateway" to using other drugs.

There's also a serious risk of DXM poisoning. If you take a high dose of cold medicine to get the DXM, you are also taking a high dose of all the other chemicals that come with it. High doses of antihistamines, for example, can cause blood pressure to drop to dangerous levels, while decongestants can raise blood pressure too high. Many DXM medications include acetaminophen (Tylenol), which can severely damage the liver if taken at high doses. And, again, there is the risk of mixing DXM with alcohol

DXM AND THE LAW

When used correctly, DXM is a safe and effective medication. Concerns about recreational use of DXM—which is sometimes called "robo-tripping" because of the drug's association with Robitussin—inspired lawmakers to regulate access to the drug.

or other party drugs. One study estimated that of all emergency room visits related to DXM use, about one-third involved combining DXM with alcohol.

Most worrying, though, may be the risk of long-term damage to even casual DXM users. For example, researchers believe that the ability to form memories may be affected by repeated DXM use. Teenagers are at greater risk for these problems because their brains are still developing. Users are also at high risk of injuring themselves or others because their vision is impaired.

Last but not least, DXM has become increasingly available in a "pure" form. It is sold on the Internet in powder and tablet forms. This is a legal product, but it's vital to understand that the dosages of "pure DXM" are extraordinarily high. A user would ingest far more DXM in a few "98 percent pure tablets" than by, for example, drinking an entire bottle of cough medicine. At these dosages, DXM does, in fact, have the ability to kill.

PSEUDOEPHEDRINE

In chapter one, a distinction was drawn between the two main types of medications: those that are available over the counter and those that only available by prescription. But in fact there is a third type: "behind-the-counter" drugs. These drugs can be purchased without a prescription, but the customer has to approach the counter and ask for them. Often, sales are restricted to people over 18, and sometimes the store is even obligated

HEALTH WARNING: ANTIDEPRESSANTS

Over-the-counter drugs are approved by the Food and Drug Administration (FDA) as being safe to consume. But that assurance refers to taking the drugs *as directed*. It does not mean that the medicines are safe for all people at all dosages. In particular, people who take other medications on a regular basis need to be very careful about what OTC drugs they consume.

For example, cold and cough medicines, including pseudoephedrine, ephedrine, and DXM, can all interact with antidepressants (like Prozac and Cipramil) in very dangerous ways. Pseudoephedrine combined with an antidepressant can cause a significant increase in blood pressure. DXM, on the other hand, can contribute to severe depression or (depending on the person) severe excitability if combined with an antidepressant. If you are on a regularly prescribed medication, be sure you know the facts about which OTCs are safe to take and which are not.

If you are taking antidepressants, talk to your doctor or pharmacist to make sure you know what OTC drugs are safe for you.

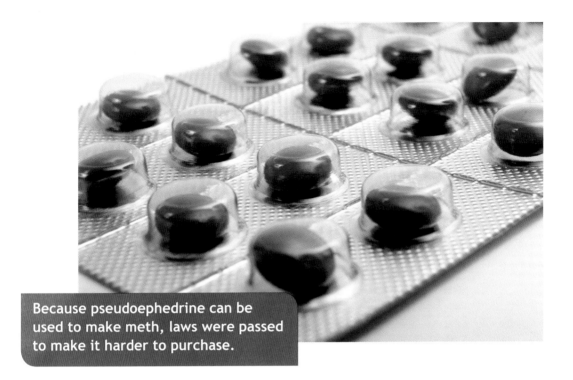

Because pseudoephedrine can be used to make meth, laws were passed to make it harder to purchase.

to write down the contact information of whoever buys the drug. One "behind-the-counter" drug is called pseudoephedrine.

Ephedra is a type of plant that has been used in traditional Chinese medicine for thousands of years. (A component of the plant, called ephedrine, is itself a frequently abused drug and is discussed in chapter three.) Pseudoephedrine replicates the medical properties of ephedra, but it is created in a laboratory. It is the main ingredient in cold and sinus medications like Sudafed, Advil Cold and Sinus, and others.

These medicines are abused because they are **stimulants**. They speed up certain bodily functions, such as heart rate. They also lead to an increase in the brain's production of a substance called dopamine, which is part of the brain's "reward pathway." Artificially raising dopamine levels can interrupt normal functioning of the brain and result in dependence or addiction.

As far as stimulants go, pseudoephedrine is one of the milder ones, which is why it is available for sale without a prescription. (See the sidebar for an important health warning, however!) There are two main concerns about it. First, experimenting with pseudoephedrine can lead people, especially kids, to misuse more serious and addictive stimulants later.

Second, and most importantly, pseudoephedrine is an ingredient in methamphetamine, or meth. Meth is a highly addictive illegal stimulant that is considered to be a scourge on many communities. It is created, or "cooked," in labs, and pseudoephedrine is a key component in that process. Concerns about this connection led the U.S. Congress to pass the Combat Methamphetamine Epidemic Act of 2005. The law requires that people must have ID in order to purchase drugs containing pseudoephedrine, and it also limits how much individuals can purchase every month. (For more on the meth issue, please see the book *Stimulants* in this set.)

TEXT-DEPENDENT QUESTIONS

1. What part of your body does cough medicine affect?
2. What are "behind-the-counter" drugs, and why are they regulated this way?
3. What are some of the physical risks of DXM abuse?

RESEARCH PROJECT

Study the graphics found in the NIH publication "Drug Facts: High School and Youth Trends," which can be found at http://www.drugabuse.gov/publications/drugfacts/high-school-youth-trends. Pick one of the graphics and write a paragraph or two describing the information presented and its importance.

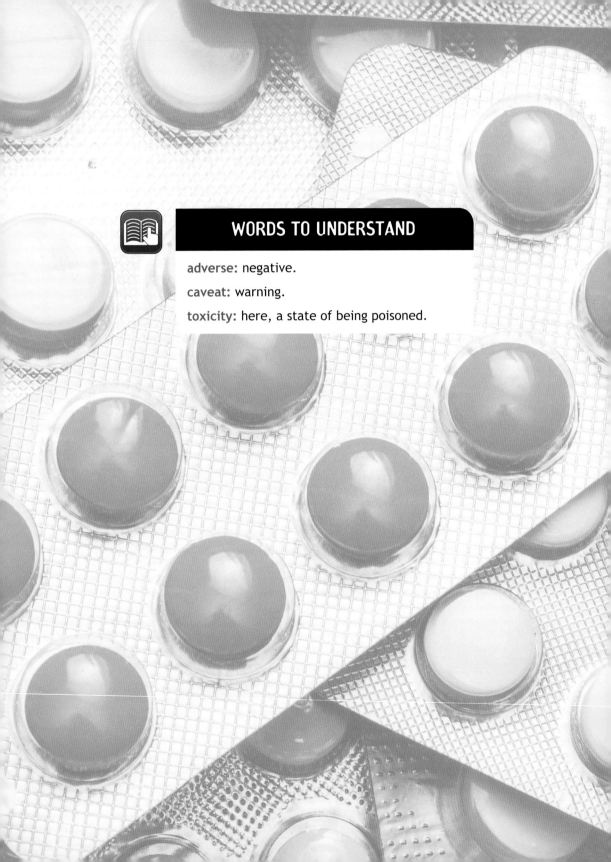

WORDS TO UNDERSTAND

adverse: negative.

caveat: warning.

toxicity: here, a state of being poisoned.

CHAPTER THREE

ENERGY DRINKS AND CAFFEINE PRODUCTS

In the previous chapter, it was noted that a plant known as ephedra has been used in Chinese medicine for thousands of years. There is another stimulant with just as long a history: caffeine.

From the Ethiopian goat herder who (according to legend) discovered the coffee plant, to the Chinese emperor who supposedly discovered tea when leaves fell into his royal water, caffeinated beverages have a long and storied history. Today, about 80 percent of Americans consume caffeine regularly. Caffeine is also added to some OTC medications, such as the headache remedy called Excedrin, and it is also an ingredient in many of the supplements discussed in chapter four.

In moderation, caffeine is considered quite safe—in fact, some products with caffeine are believed to have health benefits. Nevertheless, caffeine is an intense stimulant, especially at high doses. Often, it's the *mixing* of caffeine with other drugs that causes concern, such as when high doses of caffeine are combined with another stimulant like ephedra, or when caffeine is blended into alcoholic drinks.

HOW DOES CAFFEINE WORK?

To understand how caffeine keeps people awake, it helps to understand how they become tired in the first place. The human body has a clever way of making sure that it gets rest: as cells go about their regular processes, they also release a substance called adenosine. The brain has special receptors that pick up the adenosine molecules, and the presence of adenosine signals the brain that the body is becoming tired. The more adenosine the brain takes in, the more tired the person becomes.

When someone drinks coffee, the coffee is digested and the caffeine enters the blood stream through the stomach and (primarily) the intestines. This is why it takes a little while for the caffeine to "kick in"—the chemical needs to travel from the gastrointestinal system to the blood stream and then to the brain. Once in the brain, the caffeine molecules attach to the adenosine receptors. Since

Coffee beans are created from the berries of the *Coffea* plant.

Adenosine signals the brain that the body needs sleep.

the adenosine is prevented from reaching the receptors, the person feels less tired.

Caffeine is dose dependent, which means that the more people take, the stronger a reaction they will have. According to the book *Buzzed*, 200 milligrams of caffeine (1 or 2 cups of strong coffee) will cause heightened brain activity, while 500 milligrams will increase heart rate by as much as 20 beats per minute, and will also cause the constriction of blood vessels.

Over time, the brain of a person who consumes caffeine regularly will actually change—it will grow additional adenosine receptors. This is why people develop a tolerance to caffeine, meaning that they need more caffeine to achieve the same feeling they used to. It also is why someone who uses caffeine on a daily basis will feel so tired if he suddenly stops.

IS CAFFEINE ADDICTIVE?

Widespread use of caffeine has led many people to question if it's truly addictive. Do many people feel useless without that first cup of coffee? Sure, but according to this view, their need for caffeine will never be "bad enough" to rise to the level of a true addiction in the medical sense. It's unlikely that there has ever been a case of someone losing his job or destroying his relationships because of his excessive soda habit.

However, caffeine does have addictive properties. People who drink significant amounts of caffeine on a regular basis can expect some adverse reactions if they stop, including headache, tiredness, irritability, or even depression. In general, people bounce back from the physical withdrawal symptoms in a few days or so. The emotional reliance on caffeine—that sense that you "just don't feel right" if you skip your morning ritual—is harder for some people to overcome. This is particularly an issue if the person has some other condition—such as a heart problem—that make caffeine dangerous.

Doctors use a book called the *Diagnostic and Statistical Manual of Mental Disorders* (DSM) as a guide for diagnosing psychological problems, including dependence disorders. The manual has been revised a number of times over the years, and the current version is

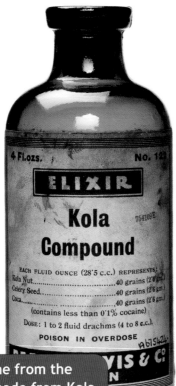

This medicine from the 1920s was made from Kola nuts. Like coffee plants, the active ingredient in kola nuts is caffeine.

called the *DSM-5*, because this is the fifth revision. The *DSM-5* does include "caffeine withdrawal" and "caffeine intoxication" as legitimate medical conditions. However, the manual stops short of declaring them a true substance use disorder, and instead notes that caffeine dependence merits more investigation.

TYPES OF PRODUCTS

It's important to understand that there can be a huge variance in how much caffeine is in particular products, even if the products seem similar. For example, analysis by the Center for Science in the Public Interest found that 16 fluid ounces of McDonald's regular coffee has 133 milligrams of caffeine, while the same amount of regular coffee from Starbucks has 330 milligrams.

So-called energy drinks have about twice as much caffeine as soda, and about the same amount as coffee. Some popular brands, like Monster Energy and Rockstar, have around 160 milligrams of caffeine in 16 ounces. The caffeine levels in a can of Red Bull are similar, but the cans are smaller; this means that Red Bull packs in more caffeine per ounce. One energy drink called Bang contains 357 milligrams of caffeine in a 16 ounce can—more than twice as much as most energy drinks. While coffee tends to be sipped, these drinks tend to be consumed quickly, which can make people feel more intensely stimulated.

DRINKER BEWARE

Unlike the other OTC drugs discussed in this book, which are dangerous when misused over time, caffeine misuse can have unpleasant side effects (like upset stomach, nervousness, or anxiety), but it is not dangerous in most cases. There are some important exceptions, though. Caffeine

Energy drinks for sale in Los Angeles.

poisoning (or **toxicity**) can occur in a small number of cases—usually because someone is taking medication that contains caffeine and then piles more caffeine on top of that. Caffeine powder is another source of caffeine toxicity (see sidebar).

Young children should not go anywhere near energy drinks, because their bodies are too small to process those levels of caffeine safely. According to the American Heart Association, out of more than 10,000 reported cases of "adverse effects" from energy drinks, 40 percent involved children under the age of six.

Frequently, the dangers of caffeine products are caused not so much by the products themselves, but by everything else that *surrounds* their use. For instance, energy drinks like Red Bull have become extremely popular party drinks mixed with alcohol. There are also premixed products called "caffeinated alcoholic beverages" (CABs) that combine the two, sometimes with other stimulants as well. And—this is important—these CABs usually do not report how much caffeine is actually in the product.

The biggest danger of mixing alcohol with energy drinks is that caffeine masks the depressant effects of alcohol. Typically, the depressant effects of alcohol force people to stop drinking before they hurt themselves—in other words, they pass out. CABs allow people to stay awake and party longer, so that people stay awake and continue drinking alcohol long after they would have passed out under normal circumstances. There are a number of frightening possible outcomes to this situation. One, of course, is alcohol

DEADLY POWDER

Some of us seem to be hardwired to believe that, "if a little is good, a lot is better." This is where troubles with caffeine can begin. Nowhere is this more evident than in the increasing use of synthetic caffeine powder, which is sold on the Internet as a supplement. The amount of caffeine in these powders is almost beyond belief: a single teaspoon of caffeine powder is equal to 16 to 25 cups of coffee. Even product manufacturers admit that a "safe" dosage is only 1/16th of a teaspoon—a miniscule amount that in the cooking world is known as, simply, a "pinch."

After an Ohio teenager died from an accidental overdose of caffeine powder in 2014, politicians at both the state and federal level began working to ban the sale of caffeine powder. However, as seen with the supplement ephedra (see chapter four), the law can only do so much.

ATHLETES AND CAFFEINE

Many athletes swear by caffeine as a way of improving their performance. Some use energy drinks like Red Bull, while others rub caffeine gels on their muscles. Do these techniques work or are they a myth? The answer is, yes, multiple studies have shown that caffeine does have a positive impact on performance. But that impact tends to be mild, not major—it's an aid, not a miracle drug. And there are a few other caveats.

Many of the foods and beverages that contain high levels of caffeine also have high levels of sugar and/or fat. Athletes need to be careful that they are not sabotaging their healthy diets with sugary caffeine supplements. Also, keep in mind what we said about tolerance: if an athlete depends on a shot of caffeine before every practice or competition, over time it will get harder and harder to get the same boost with the same amount of chemicals.

The American College of Sports Medicine (ACSM) has raised ethical questions about caffeine. In an official statement, the ACSM wondered whether adding caffeine to athletic workouts contributes to the "doping mentality" that many sports lovers would prefer to eliminate.

One downside of energy drinks is that many contain added sugar.

poisoning. Also, the alert feeling that people get from energy drinks can make it hard for people to realize how drunk they are. Consequently, studies have found that people who mix energy drinks and alcohol are more likely to be involved in "high-risk behaviors" such as driving while intoxicated. What's more, a 2008 study in the *Journal of Emergency Medicine* found that college students who had mixed the two substances were *twice as likely* to either be sexually assaulted or to sexually assault someone else.

TEXT-DEPENDENT QUESTIONS

1. What do doctors say about whether caffeine is addictive?
2. Who should never consume energy drinks?
3. What are the possible outcomes of mixing alcohol and caffeine drinks?

RESEARCH PROJECT

Find out how the different caffeine levels in various products. The Center for Science in the Public Interest has a good list (http://www.cspinet.org/new/cafchart.htm), and others are available on the Internet. Create a bar graph or table that represents caffeine levels in a visual way. Be sure to pay attention to not just the amount of caffeine, but also the serving size.

WORDS TO UNDERSTAND

laxatives: substances that cause the user to have more bowel movements.

psychosis: a mental disorder in which someone loses touch with reality.

purgatives: substances that cause the user to vomit.

suppressant: something that limits or holds back something else.

CHAPTER FOUR

DIET PILLS AND SUPPLEMENTS

It's rare to find people who can't find a single thing they'd like to change about their bodies. Even superstar athletes and celebrities still have moments of wanting to be thinner, or stronger, or more "cut." And because we're human, we'd like those changes to happen as quickly as possible, with minimal pain and suffering. This is why diet pills and nutritional supplements are so popular. In 2010, Americans spent $40 billion on weight-loss products alone—that's not counting millions more on other types of athletic supplements.

Do these products work? That's a difficult question. The answer depends on the specific product, but it also depends on the time frame you're talking about. That is, yes, diet pills might cause some weight loss over a very short period, but as soon as you stop taking the drug, the weight comes back. Unfortunately, many of these products are lightly regulated or not regulated at all; this means there is no official agency looking closely at what they contain. People who start out just wanting a

At some point in their lives, everyone has felt that they do not look "good enough" in one way or another.

little help with their waistlines or workouts can end up with more trouble than they bargained for.

DIET PILLS

Attempts at quick weight loss go all the way back to ancient Greeks, who used to take herbal laxatives and purgatives to lose weight. In the 19th century, there were many dubious products available for weight loss— they were usually called "fat reducers" at the time. Some were made to boost the thyroid, a gland in the neck that secretes hormones that can impact weight gain or loss. Others were just stimulants, which help suppress appetite.

Originally created as a decongestant, formulations of amphetamine have been used to treat a variety of problems, including mild depression and a sleep disorder called narcolepsy. During World War II, militaries on all sides of the conflict distributed amphetamines to soldiers on a regular

DNP

The search for a "magic bullet" for weight loss began with amphetamines, but it certainly didn't end there. For instance, a chemical called dinitrophenol (DNP) was invented about the same time as amphetamines and was briefly popular as a diet drug in the 1930s— until it became apparent that DNP could cause blindness, severe heart problems, and even death. These days, DNP is considered an industrial chemical that has been used in making dyes and as a pesticide. But amazingly, DNP is still sold on the Internet as a diet aid, despite wide agreement among doctors that it is extremely toxic. A 23-year-old British woman named Sarah Houston died in August 2015 after mixing DNP with her antidepressant medication.

basis. By the time the war ended, an estimated 16 million Americans had some experience with amphetamine use during their military service. Meanwhile, on the homefront, amphetamines were already being used as diet aids—one popular formula mixed a thyroid booster with a few milligrams of amphetamine.

Problems with amphetamine dependence and misuse became apparent almost immediately. A 1958 study of "amphetamine psychosis" inspired a greater focus on the problem, and the U.S. Congress held a series of hearings on the issue in the 1960s. But it wasn't until 1970 that amphetamines (including for diet use) were declared Schedule II drugs in the United States. (Schedule II drugs are much more strictly controlled and require a new prescription be written each time the patient needs more.)

While amphetamine itself is no longer used for dieting, stimulants remain a very common ingredient in diet pills. If you see an advertisement for something called an "appetite suppressant," you can assume that there is some form of stimulant in it. Because stimulants provoke a dopamine response, there is a high risk of dependency. Symptoms of diet pill misuse include headaches, vomiting, insomnia, increased heart rate, chest pain, and blackouts. Diet pills can also do damage to important organs like the

ANNUAL DIET PILL USAGE AMONG TEENS (percentage)

	1990	1995	2000	2005	2010	2014
Males	4.3	3.5	4.0	6.0	2.4	3.7
Females	16.7	15.1	15.7	13.2	6.0	8.6

Source: Monitoring the Future, 2014. http://www.monitoringthefuture.org/.

In the annual Monitoring the Future survey, high school students are asked whether they had used diet pills in the previous 12 months. After a steady drop among girls in the early 2000s, the percentage who had used diet pills in the past year crept up slightly in 2014.

DO I HAVE A PROBLEM?

Oftentimes, drug misuse is much more obvious to other people than it is to the user. Users often tell themselves that their drug use is "not a big deal," or that "I can stop any time, I just don't want to." If you use an OTC drug regularly, here are some questions that are worth asking yourself:

- Do I use the drug every day?
- Do I spend time making sure I have a supply?
- Do I feel lousy or upset if I can't get any?
- Have I ever done something I know is dangerous or stupid, just to get the drug?
- Do I need the drug to "get through the day" or "feel normal"?

Answering yes to any of these questions does not mean you *definitely* have a problem, but it does suggest a strong potential for an addiction to develop if it hasn't already. Find someone knowledgeable you can trust—be it a parent, teacher, doctor, or counselor—who can help you look closely at your answers to these questions and decide what to do next.

liver and kidneys. Teenage girls tend to be at the greatest risk of diet pill dependency, and they are also the major users of diet pills. A University of Minnesota study found that 20 percent of young women had used diet pills by the time they were 20 years old.

EPHEDRA

For thousands of years, healers in China and India have been using an herb called *ma huang* to cure a variety of problems such as fever, cough, and headache. In the West, common varieties of the plant include *Ephedra sinica*, *Ephedra equisetina*, and *Ephedra intermedia*. The medically useful chemical in the ephedra plant is called *ephedrine*, a central nervous system

(CNS) stimulant. Certain ephedrine-based compounds called alkaloids are common in cold medicines (see chapter two for a discussion on pseudoephedrine). These alkaloids all work in similar ways and have been used to treat sinus problems, cold symptoms, and sleep disorders, among other problems. Ephedrine alkaloids are extremely good at those jobs.

But since the 1970s, ephedra has found another home in the less-regulated world of diet pills and nutritional supplements. Products including ephedra make a large range of claims, such as improving mood, building muscle, and promoting weight loss. Ephedrine-containing products are sometimes sold as "herbal ecstasy." Supposedly, these products offer a mood-altering experience similar to the drug ecstasy, but without any of the dangers because they are "herbal."

Despite these claims, ephedrine is not particularly good at any of these jobs. Research shows that ephedrine does not impact the brain or alter mood very effectively. Because it increases heart rate, blood pressure, and glucose levels, users experience a heightened "jumpy" sensation that can

The stimulant properties of ephedra supplements may just be tricking you into *thinking* you are having a better-than-usual workout.

be mistaken for a high, but it is actually nothing like the high associated with ecstasy. And it's important to remember that slapping the name "herbal" on something does not necessarily guarantee that the product is truly "natural" or even safe.

There are a lot of questions about how well ephedra even works. The increased heart rate and related physical effects

The herb *ma huang*, used in traditional Chinese medicine.

make people feel like they are having a great workout, but scientific data suggests that ephedrine is fairly ineffective at stimulating muscle growth. Finally, claims that the drug "melts fat away" are not to be trusted. One study found that ephedrine products combined with caffeine resulted in an average loss of five pounds in two months. Most people can lose that amount of weight by cutting calories and going to the gym.

Because nutritional supplements are not regulated the way normal medicines are, users have no way of knowing how much ephedra is actually in any given product. One study of ephedra products found that some contained 20 percent more ephedra *inside* the bottle than was advertised on the outside; even different bottles of the same products were found to have varying amounts. This means it's easy to overdose on ephedra *even if you carefully follow dosage instructions*.

This is why the Food and Drug Administration (FDA) banned the sale of nutritional supplements containing ephedrine in 2004. In a statement, the secretary of health and human services said, "This FDA rule reflects what the scientific evidence shows—that ephedra poses an unreasonable risk to those who use it." Supplement makers fought the ban hard, but it was upheld by the courts in 2006. However, some companies continue to sell

DON'T BELIEVE THE HYPE

Over the years, lawsuits about false advertising have revealed that there are a number of standard tricks used by some companies that sell diet pills and supplements to convince people to try their products.

For example, a lot of the advertisements feature "before" and "after" photos, supposedly to provide evidence that the product can transform the ugly duckling in the first photo into the beautiful swan in the second. But some people who've posed for those ads say that many deceptive practices were used. For example, one woman admitted that she had been pregnant when the "before" photo was taken. A man who posed for another photo said that he was given a food budget and told to eat as much as possible in anticipation of the "before" photo shoot.

Another trick companies use is doctor endorsements. One company was caught suggesting that a chiropractor (who is by definition not

a medical doctor) was qualified to endorse a diet aid. In another case, a lawsuit revealed that the doctors paid to "endorse" a particular product had never actually prescribed the pill to their patients.

Weight-loss companies have lots of tricks to make their "before/after" advertisements look more convincing.

"ephedra" products online. Some are doing this illegally, while others claim that the FDA does not apply because they are using parts of the ephedra plant that don't contain ephedrine. According to *Consumer Reports*, these new formulations may be legal, but they are totally ineffective.

TEXT-DEPENDENT QUESTIONS

1. What are the symptoms of diet pill abuse?
2. What are some of the physical dangers of ephedra?
3. What tricks do some nutritional supplement advertisements use to make their product look better?

RESEARCH PROJECT

Look critically at a nutritional supplement advertisement on the Internet (for example, on YouTube). Listen carefully to the claims and create a list of whatever you find questionable. For example, does the advertisement claim some kind of "magic" short-term weight loss with little effort required? What proof, if any, does the advertisement offer? Does the ad include testimonials from people who claim to have had success with the product? If so, how do you know you can believe them? Does a doctor recommend the product, and if so, what kind of academic background does he or she have?

WORDS TO UNDERSTAND

dilate: to make wider.

dopamine: a type of brain chemical.

inhibitions: self-conscious feelings that keep you from behaving as you might like to.

neurological: having to do with the brain and nervous system.

solvent: a type of liquid that is used for dissolving other things.

vapor: molecules of a substance suspended in air; such as water vapor.

volatile: changing easily.

CHAPTER FIVE

INHALANTS

Right now, stop reading for just a second and picture someone "doing drugs." What did you see? Maybe you pictured a person smoking or injecting something. Or maybe you imagined someone swallowing pills, or drinking alcohol. Chances are, the first image that came into your head was not a person just sniffing something that he or she could purchase over the counter.

But in fact, inhalants—as sniffable drugs are called—are a popular and dangerous way of getting high, especially among younger kids. Sometimes this is called "huffing," "bagging," or "glading." According to the National Survey on Drug Use and Health from 2010, about 800,000 people tried inhalants for the first time that year, 68.4 percent of whom were under the age of 18.

WHAT ARE INHALANTS?

The term *inhalant* is a catchall word for many different types of chemicals and products that produce vapors that can enter the bloodstream through

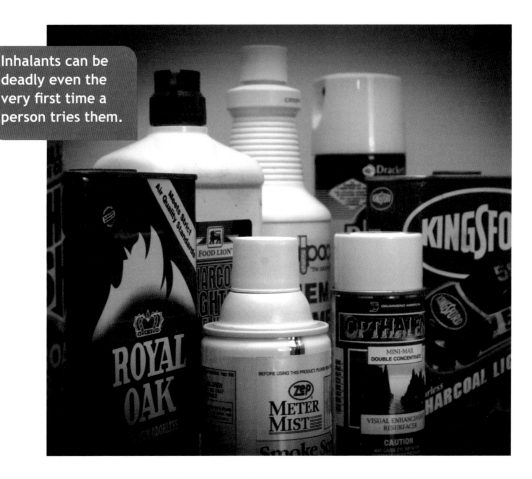

Inhalants can be deadly even the very first time a person tries them.

the nasal passages. Inhalants—including paint thinner, gasoline, and whipped cream cans—are usually products with legitimate uses. But when inhaled, they can cause a quick and addictive "high."

To understand what inhalants are, it might help to recall some very basic science. There are three states of matter that are relevant: solid, liquid, and gas (or **vapor**). (There's also a fourth state of matter, plasma, but it is not relevant to this discussion.) It's easy to think of the states of matter as being stable—you might say, for example, that solid rock is always solid rock. But if you think about water, it's easy to see how quickly some forms of matter can go from one state to another. Sure, an ice cube is a solid, but it can be melted into liquid and then boiled into vapor.

If you go the gas station to fill up your car, the pump will deliver gasoline into the tank in liquid form. But if you breathe deeply anywhere around a gas station, you will smell the gas. That's vapor, and the chemicals in gasoline vapor are not significantly different from the chemicals in liquid gasoline. There are more than 150 different chemicals in gasoline, many of them toxic. If you're thinking about inhaling gasoline to get high (and people do!), you might ask yourself: do I really want to put the same toxic chemicals in my body that I'd put in a car?

There are almost too many inhalant drugs to count, but they can be grouped into four broad types:

- *Volatile substances*, like gasoline, turn to vapor very easily, even at room temperature. Some of the volatile liquids that people use as inhalants are also solvents, such as turpentine, paint thinner, and degreaser. For that reason, these types of inhalants are sometimes referred to as "volatile solvents." But in fact there are many volatile liquids that aren't solvents but that can be abused—like glue and the ink in magic markers.

- *Aerosols* are liquids that are sold in pressurized cans. The pressure is used to break the liquid into tiny particles that can be sprayed easily. But they can also be inhaled: spray paints, deodorants, and hair sprays are all aerosols that some people use as inhalants.

- *Gases*, on the other hand, are designed and sold in that form. Sometimes inhalable gases are intended for medical purposes, such as the nitrous oxide ("laughing gas") that dentists frequently use to calm their patients. There are other gases—including the butane in lighters, propane fuel, and refrigerants—that are intended for legitimate purposes but misused as inhalants. The most popular inhalant in this category by far is the nitrous oxide that's sold in whipped cream cans, nicknamed "whip-its."

WHO ARE INHALANT USERS?

Users of inhalants tend to be younger and poorer than users of almost any other drug. According to a 2010 report by the Canadian Paediatric Society, inhalant use is more common among kids who are abused, neglected, or homeless, as well as among teens who have dropped out of school or been incarcerated. Kids from lower socioeconomic backgrounds, whose parents have less education and lower incomes, tend to be more likely to use inhalants than other kids.

This is not to say that kids from more privileged backgrounds do not use drugs. The point is that their choice of drug tends to be different. Partly this is a question of availability. Even cigarettes, these days, are more expensive than many products that can be inhaled.

Inhalant abuse is not at all unique to the United States. Karachi is Pakistan's largest city, and one study estimated that among the city's street kids—who may number as many as 14,000—rates of inhalant use are around 90 percent. A similar observation has been made about homeless youth in Nairobi, Kenya. The Canadian report theorizes that children in developing countries use inhalants to mask their feelings of hunger.

- *Nitrites* are a special category of inhalants. More frequently used by adults, nitrites **dilate** blood vessels. One type, called amyl nitrite ("poppers"), is used as a party drug to stimulate sexual activity. Amyl nitrite was invented in the 19th century as a treatment for chest pain. But its real popularity is associated with the 1970s disco era, followed by a resurgence in the 1990s during the "rave" era.

WHAT DO INHALANTS DO?

The precise effects of inhalants vary, depending on their chemical composition. With the exception of nitrites, all inhalants work by slowing down the central nervous system (CNS). The CNS is composed of the brain and the spinal cord—it controls all kinds of vital functions, including thinking, moving, and breathing. Anything that interferes with the CNS— as many medications and all inhalants do—has to be taken very seriously, because the costs of CNS malfunction can be extremely high.

A great many inhalants also have something else in common: the presence of a chemical called toluene. Toluene is a chemical that, researchers believe, triggers a dopamine response in the brain. Dopamine is part of the brain's "reward pathway," so that things that trigger an increase in dopamine are things that we tend to want to do again. This is a big part of why drugs—including inhalants—can be so attractive and habit forming.

One issue with inhalants is that the "high" only lasts for a very short time. It's common for kids to think this means that it is really not a big deal. After all, whatever effect you might feel from an inhalant will be gone in a matter of minutes. There's a few problems with that line of thought. The first is that just because the good feeling is gone, that doesn't mean the toxic chemicals are gone from your body. Second, the short high leads kids to use again right away, and again and again. Each exposure amplifies the effect of the previous one.

WHAT'S THE BIG DEAL?

Using inhalants feels a bit like using alcohol: There is a lightheaded, "fuzzy" sensation, and there can be some dizziness and a lowering of inhibitions. But there are lots of differences between inhalants and

HAZARDS

Risks of Hazardous Chemicals Found in Commonly Abused Inhalants

- **Amyl nitrite, butyl nitrite** *("poppers," "video head cleaner")*: sudden sniffing death syndrome, suppressed immunologic function, injury to red blood cells (interfering with oxygen supply to vital tissues)

- **benzene** *(found in gasoline)*: bone marrow injury, impaired immunologic function, increased risk of leukemia, reproductive system toxicity

- **butane, propane** *(found in lighter fluid, hair and paint sprays)*: sudden sniffing death syndrome via cardiac effects, serious burn injuries (because of flammability)

- **freon** *(used as a refrigerant and aerosol propellant)*: sudden sniffing death syndrome, respiratory obstruction and death (from sudden cooling/cold injury to airways), liver damage

- **methylene chloride** *(found in paint thinners and removers, degreasers)*: reduction of oxygen-carrying capacity of blood, changes to the heart muscle and heartbeat

- **nitrous oxide** *("laughing gas")*: death from lack of oxygen to the brain, altered perception and motor coordination, loss of sensation, limb spasms, blackouts caused by blood pressure changes, depression of heart muscle functioning

- **toluene** *(found in gasoline, paint thinners and removers, correction fluid)*: brain damage (loss of brain tissue mass, impaired cognition, gait disturbance, loss of coordination, loss of equilibrium, limb spasms, hearing and vision loss), liver and kidney damage

- **trichloroethylene** *(found in spot removers, degreasers)*: sudden sniffing death syndrome, cirrhosis of the liver, reproductive complications, hearing and vision damage

Source: National Institute on Drug Abuse, *Inhalants* (Research Report Series). http://www.drugabuse.gov/publications/research-reports/inhalants/what-are-other-medical-consequences-inhalant-abuse.

alcohol—and between inhalants and the other OTC drugs discussed in this volume. The most significant difference is that alcohol and other OTC drugs will almost never kill someone the first time they use it. That can't be said about inhalants.

The expression *sudden sniffing death syndrome* (SSDS) sounds a little like something a doctor invented to frighten patients. But SSDS is no myth. It's the real term for cardiac arrest—the sudden stopping of the heart— after using inhalants. Sometimes the problem is caused by the chemicals themselves; other times it happens when an inhalant user engages in rigorous activity right after inhaling. A perfectly healthy person can be gone in an instant due to SSDS.

For those fortunate enough to avoid SSDS, the chemicals in inhalants can cause seizures, convulsions, and irreversible damage to the kidneys, liver, and brain. It's also possible to choke or suffocate while inhaling. The longer a person uses inhalants, the more likely he or she will experience permanent effects such as memory loss, attention problems, and learning difficulties. Symptoms of the **neurological** disease called Parkinson's can actually be brought on by long-term inhalant abuse.

As with many other drugs, sometimes the greatest dangers are not the drug itself, but the decisions that people make while high. Driving under the influence of inhalants is no safer than driving while drunk. And again, it only takes one mistake.

INHALANT ADDICTION?

Inhalants are not as widely studied as many other addictive drugs. One result is that reliable numbers on inhalant dependency are difficult to find. We know from surveys that about 1 in 5 eighth graders has tried an inhalant at some point. But that doesn't tell us anything when it comes to addiction or dependence. However, any chemical that provokes a dopamine response

HELIUM

If you've been to a party, you've been around helium balloons. And if you've been around helium balloons, at some point, somebody has untied one and breathed in the helium to make his voice sound strange. You may also have seen this on TV, the Internet, or even in your own science class, because some teachers use helium balloons to demonstrate the effects of an invisible gas.

While this trick is pretty common and definitely funny, it's actually not completely safe. Pure helium actually removes oxygen from the lungs. That means your oxygen level is dropping much faster than it would by just holding your breath—you are actively losing oxygen as you breathe in helium.

Usually, breathing in a little helium from a balloon won't do anything worse than make you lightheaded. As long as you don't fall over and hurt yourself (which can and does happen!), you're unlikely to suffer any long term effects. But some thrill-seekers breathe helium directly out of tanks, and this is where things can get scary. A balloon only provides

a limited amount of helium with some ambient air mixed in. A pressurized tank can fill lungs with pure helium very quickly. In some instances, this can cause the lungs to collapse. A stunt involving climbing into a giant helium balloon has killed several college students in the United States and has also been reported in Japan.

Helium removes oxygen from the lungs, which is why it can be dangerous in large quantities.

is likely to inspire dependent behavior. Plus, inhalants tend to be cheap and easy to find—there are dozens in any given grocery or hardware store. This can make inhalants both tempting to try and difficult to get away from. Users often experience psychological dependency on inhalants, and crave them when the drugs are not available. Symptoms of dependency include anxiety, irritability, aggression, tremors, and dizziness.

Not all treatment programs are equipped to deal with inhalant dependency, but programs do exist. Check the resources in the back of this book for places to start.

TEXT-DEPENDENT QUESTIONS

1. What are the main categories of inhalants?
2. What does SSDS stand for, and what causes it?
3. What are some of the toxic chemicals in inhalants, and what are the risks of inhaling them?

RESEARCH PROJECT

Pick one common inhalant to research. Make a list of all its ingredients and their chemical effects.

FURTHER READING

BOOKS

Flynn, Noa. *Inhalants and Solvents: Sniffing Disaster.* Broomall, PA: Mason Crest, 2013.

Hoffman, John, and Susan Froemke, eds. *Addiction: Why Can't They Just Stop?* New York: Rodale, 2007.

Kuhn, Cynthia, Scott Swartzwelder, and Wilkie Wilson. *Buzzed: The Straight Facts about the Most Used and Abused Drugs from Alcohol to Ecstasy.* 4th ed. New York: W. W. Norton, 2014.

ONLINE

Miech, Richard A., et al. *Monitoring the Future National Survey Results on Drug Use, 1975-2014.* Vol. 1, Secondary School Students. Ann Arbor: Institute for Social Research, University of Michigan, 2015. http://www.monitoringthefuture.org/pubs/monographs/mtf-vol1_2014.pdf.

National Institute on Drug Abuse. "DrugFacts: Prescription and Over-the-Counter Medications." December 2014. http://www.drugabuse.gov/publications/drugfacts/prescription-over-counter-medications.

National Institute on Drug Abuse. Inhalants. Research Report Series. http://www.drugabuse.gov/publications/research-reports/inhalants/what-are-other-medical-consequences-inhalant-abuse.

EDUCATIONAL VIDEOS

Access these videos with your smartphone or use the URLs below to find them online.

 "RoboTripping," ABC News. "DXM and its consequences." https://youtu.be/yn_nLFFmD4c

 "I See the Effects Daily," WTHI-TV. "Recovering drug offender speaks out about pseudoephedrine." https://youtu.be/RVkwXLb8YIc

 "Coffee vs. Energy Drinks: A Caffeine Wake-Up Call," Cleveland Clinic. "Dr. Nissen talks about the safety of coffee, caffeinated soft drinks and energy drinks." https://youtu.be/n1yplCDdJf4

 "Dangerous Drugs Found in Dietary Supplements," HBO Real Sports. "Dr. Pieter Cohen details what's been found in spiked supplements." https://youtu.be/-kmJCgILdVQ

 "InsideDope: Inhalants." PowerSurge Videos. "Kids no longer just sniff glue; they try everything from bug spray to household cleaners." https://youtu.be/Dg3iY4aZaSQ

SERIES GLOSSARY

abstention: actively choosing to not do something.

acute: something that is intense but lasts a short time.

alienation: a sense of isolation or detachment from a larger group.

alleviate: to lessen or relieve.

binge: doing something to excess.

carcinogenic: something that causes cancer.

chronic: ongoing or recurring.

cognitive: having to do with thought.

compulsion: a desire that is very hard or even impossible to resist.

controlled substance: a drug that is regulated by the government.

coping mechanism: a behavior a person learns or develops in order to manage stress.

craving: a very strong desire for something.

decriminalized: something that is not technically legal but is no longer subject to prosecution.

depressant: a substance that slows particular bodily functions.

detoxify: to remove toxic substances (such as drugs or alcohol) from the body.

ecosystem: a community of living things interacting with their environment.

environment: one's physical, cultural, and social surroundings.

genes: units of inheritance that are passed from parent to child and contain information about specific traits and characteristics.

hallucinate: seeing things that aren't there.

hyperconscious: to be intensely aware of something.

illicit: illegal; forbidden by law or cultural custom.

inhibit: to limit or hold back.

interfamilial: between and among members of a family.

metabolize: the ability of a living organism to chemically change compounds.

neurotransmitter: a chemical substance in the brain.

paraphernalia: the equipment used for producing or ingesting drugs, such as pipes or syringes.

physiological: relating to the way an organism functions.

placebo: a medication that has no physical effect and is used to test whether new drugs actually work.

predisposition: to be more inclined or likely to do something.

prohibition: when something is forbidden by law.

recidivism: a falling back into past behaviors, especially criminal ones.

recreation: something done for fun or enjoyment.

risk factors: behaviors, traits, or influences that make a person vulnerable to something.

sobriety: the state of refraining from alcohol or drugs.

social learning: a way that people learn behaviors by watching other people.

stimulant: a class of drug that speeds up bodily functions.

stressor: any event, thought, experience, or biological or chemical function that causes a person to feel stress.

synthetic: made by people, often to replicate something that occurs in nature.

tolerance: the state of needing more of a particular substance to achieve the same effect.

traffic: to illegally transport people, drugs, or weapons to sell throughout the world.

withdrawal: the physical and psychological effects that occur when a person with a use disorder suddenly stops using substances.

INDEX

ABOUT THE AUTHOR

H.W. Poole is a writer and editor of books for young people, such as the multivolume sets *Mental Illnesses and Disorders* and *Families in the 21st Century* (Mason Crest). She is also responsible for many critically acclaimed reference books, including *Political Handbook of the World* (CQ Press) and the *Encyclopedia of Terrorism* (SAGE). She was coauthor and editor of the *History of the Internet* (ABC-CLIO), which won the 2000 American Library Association RUSA award.

ABOUT THE ADVISOR

Sara Becker, Ph.D. is a clinical researcher and licensed clinical psychologist specializing in the treatment of adolescents with substance use disorders. She is an Assistant Professor (Research) in the Center for Alcohol and Addictions Studies at the Brown School of Public Health and the Evaluation Director of the New England Addiction Technology Transfer Center. Dr. Becker received her Ph.D. in Clinical Psychology from Duke University and completed her clinical residency at Harvard Medical School's McLean Hospital. She joined the Center for Alcohol and Addictions Studies as a postdoctoral fellow and transitioned to the faculty in 2011. Dr. Becker directs a program of research funded by the National Institute on Drug Abuse that explores novel ways to improve the treatment of adolescents with substance use disorders. She has authored over 30 peer-reviewed publications and book chapters and serves on the Editorial Board of the *Journal of Substance Abuse Treatment*.

PHOTO CREDITS